בס"ד

The whole world is Hashem's, and all that is in it.

לה' הארץ ומלואה

_____
MY NAME

HACHAI PUBLISHING

A Chanuka Story for Night Number Three

BY ME

MATISYOHU DOV BER CHAIM TZVI

As told to Dina Rosenfeld
and illustrated by Harris Mandel
Edited by Dovid Sholom Pape

I'm just a brain-child, a figment created
By my author brain-mother to whom I'm related,
She's got super parents, both really top-rated,
'And it's to them, with love, that this book's dedicated!

M.D.B.C.T.

A Chanuka Story for Night Number Three

FIRST EDITION
First Impression — SEPTEMBER 1989

Published by HaChai Publishing

ISBN 0—922613—16—8 (Casebound Edition)
ISBN 0—922613—07—6 (Softcover Edition)

Distributed by:

HaChai Distributions
705 Foster Avenue
Brooklyn, New York 11230
(718) 692-3900

Printed in Hong Kong

This publication
is made possible
by a grant from
the educational division
of the

Laboratories

My name's Matisyohu Dov Ber Chaim Tzvi,
My birthday's on Chanukah night number three.
This year something happened that I guarantee,
You'll never believe really happened to me!

I've got shopping to do, Mommy said with a smile,
"I won't be gone long, just a very short while.
Goodbye, Matisyohu Dov Ber Chaim Tzvi,
Get ready for Chanukah night number three."

The menorah was waiting with three
    wicks to light,
The table was ready, all set for that night.
I looked through the house for something to do,
When I got an idea; something great,
    something new!

Other kids on their birthdays eat plain birthday cake,
For my Chanukah birthday, a latke I'd make!
The most giant latke there ever could be,
For my birthday on Chanukah night number three!

I ran to the kitchen and found a cookbook,
And took a big apron and hat from the hook.
I peeled piles of potatoes — six hundred and nine,
For that super huge fabulous latke of mine!

I grated potatoes, and grated some more,
I grated till all of my fingers were sore!
I'd make the biggest latke you would ever see,
All for Matisyohu Dov Ber Chaim Tzvi!

I put in all the flour and eggs I could find,
I knew that my mother would surely not mind!
It's not every day that her very own son,
Is making a latke that weighs half a ton!

I turned on the mixer; it started to spin,
I took all the batter and poured it right in.
The mixer was mixing it, when… just my luck,
The beaters stopped spinning; the whole
    thing was stuck!

"Well now, Matisyohu Dov Ber Chaim Tzvi,"
I said to myself, "well, *now* what will be?"
Then I heard a loud noise. I jumped to my feet,
And I saw a cement-mixing truck on my street!

I ran outside fast in my apron and hat,
Calling, "Sir, could you mix up my batter with that?"
"Why sure, Matisyohu Dov Ber Chaim Tzvi,
Just pour it all in, and leave it to me!"

I brought out the batter in barrels and jars,
Taking care not to splash on the sidewalk or cars,
I used every bucket, each glass, bowl, and pot,
That we had in the house — There was such a lot!

I brought out the batter, and in it all went,
To the wonderful truck that mixes cement.
It mixed up the batter, made it smooth, made it fine,
For that super, huge, fabulous latke of mine!

"And now," called the man, "here's a friend you should meet,
He has a big dump truck just down the street!"
As the mixer truck poured all the batter inside
I climbed on the dump truck to go for the ride.

I sat in the batter so ushy and skwushy,
My wonderful latke was still soft and mushy.
"Oh no," I cried out, "I never can make it!
I don't have an oven big enough to bake it!"

"Don't worry," said the driver with a smile on his face,
"To make this huge latke I know just the place!
To cook up a latke, you don't bake or broil,
You fry it till crisp in a saucepan with oil.

"I'll take you and your latke and dump you both down
At the hospital kitchen, the biggest in town!
The hospital cook will know just what to do
When he sees me come in with your latke and you!"

That's just where we went, and that's just what he did,
Off of the truck with the batter, I slid.
The hospital cook took a huge copper pot,
Put my latke inside it and let it get hot.

All the hospital patients who were feeling so sad,
Sat up in their beds and stopped feeling so bad.
Together we lit the third Chanukah light,
Then looked out of the window and saw quite a sight!

The world's biggest dreidle was parked in the lot,
The cement mixer spun like a big spinning top!
The driver had painted nun, gimmel, hay, shin,
So whenever his truck spun around we could win!

I asked for attention and jumped on a chair,
I told them the Chanukah story from there,
Of the giant Greek army — the Jewish one small,
And how G-d helped the Jews win the war after all.

How they cleaned up the Temple — the menorah they lit
With some pure olive oil, the tiniest bit,
A small jar of oil — just enough for one night,
That burned for eight days with miraculous light.

"The latke is ready!" called the cook, "come and eat!"
It was light brown and crispy — the best birthday treat!
Everyone in the hospital wanted a taste,
So we served them all latke, and none went to waste!

Together we sang "Maoz Tzur Yeshuosi,"
And added, of course, "Happy birthday to me!"
A wonderful mitzva — the best there could be,
Thanks to *me,* Matisyohu Dov Ber Chaim Tzvi!

My truck driver friend drove me home after that,
Tired but happy in my apron and hat.
When I opened my door, what a mess I did see!
The batter was everywhere, even on me!

It had splattered the ceiling, the walls, and the floor,
On the tables and counters there was even more.
Sticky dishes and spoons, dirty pots in the sink,
''When Mommy gets home, I don't know what she'll think!''

"Don't worry, my friend, I think you're in luck,
I know someone else with a different type truck."
A street cleaning truck cleaned the house in a rush,
By spraying some water and twirling its brush!

"Thank you both," I called out, "Happy night number three,
From me, Matisyohu Dov Ber Chaim Tzvi!"
The truck cleaned me too, and it drove out the door,
Just as Mommy walked in; she was back from the store.

"Tell me, Matisyohu Dov Ber Chaim Tzvi,
Did anything happen at home without me?"
I told Mommy what happened all the while she was gone,
I told the whole story; I talked on and on.

"What a story!" she said, "Why not write it down?
For your father to see when he gets back from town!
So I wrote all that happened for you to read too.
If you want to believe it, well, that's up to you!

PUT CANDLES OR OIL IN——1, 2, AND 3,

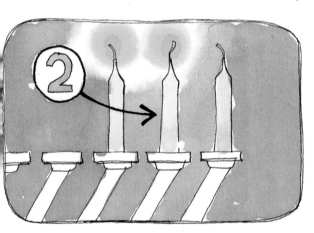 

THEN LIGHT THEM THE OTHER WAY AS YOU CAN SEE.

YOU PROBABLY GUESSED, BUT I'D JUST LIKE TO SAY,
THAT ALL THE OTHER NIGHTS WORK THE VERY SAME WAY.

NOW HERE IS ANOTHER IMPORTANT NICE THING,
THE CHANUKA BLESSINGS TO SAY OR TO SING.

Boruch Atoh Ado-noi, Elo-heinu, Melech Ho-Olom She'oso Nissim La-Avoseinu Bayomim Hoheim Bizman Hazeh.
Blessed are You, L-rd our G-d, King of the universe, who performed miracles for our forefathers in those days, at this time.
After saying the blessings, we light the candles, from left to right.

The first time we light, we also say:
Boruch Atoh Ado-noi Elo-heinu Melech Ho-Olom Shehecheyonu V-Kiyimonu V-Higiyonu Lizman Hazeh.
Blessed are You, L-rd our G-d, King of the universe, who has kept us alive, sustained us, and enabled us to reach this occasion.

Also Available Through
HACHAI PUBLISHING

Written by **Dina Rosenfeld**
Illustrated by **Amir Zelcer**

Goodnight
My Friend Aleph

Written & Illustrated
by Tova Mordechai

Take Care Of Me

Written by Chana Rivka Jacobs
Illustrated by Amir Zelcer
Edited by Dina Rosenfeld

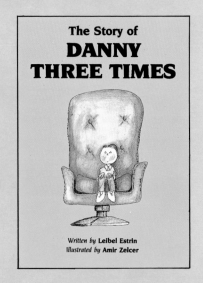

The Story of
**DANNY
THREE TIMES**

Written by **Leibel Estrin**
Illustrated by **Amir Zelcer**

A
Little Boy
Named Avram
By Dina Rosenfeld

Drawings by Ilene Winn-Lederer

A New Experience
in Children's Literature